BECOME TH
YOUR TEA

YOU
GO
FIRST

RONDA CONGER

You Go First: *Become the Leader Your Team Needs*
By Ronda Conger © 2018

Print ISBN: 978-1-61206-151-1
eBook ISBN: 978-1-61206-152-8

Interior and Cover Design by: inJoy Design, inJoy-Design.com
Editorial Team: Anna McHargue and Holly Haener

Google and the Google logo are registered trademarks of Google Inc., used with permission.

For more information, visit YouGoFirst.com.

This book may be purchased in bulk for educational, business, organizational or promotional
use. For discounted pricing, go to AlohaPublishing.com or email alohapublishing@gmail.com.

Published by

ALOHA
PUBLISHING

AlohaPublishing.com

Printed in the United States of America

To my sons,
Bailey and Cooper

You inspire me

Contents

INTRODUCTION

I was raised with the quote "If you're not the lead dog, the view never changes."

The leaders in my early childhood were a mixed bag. Some good. Some bad. I needed both.

They inspired me. They showed what I did—and did *not*—want to be. It was clear that I was looking for something, and that something wouldn't be found at home. It had to be sought elsewhere. So that's what I did. I started searching. I looked for people and leaders worth following.

I KNEW I WANTED MY VIEW TO CHANGE AND THE ONLY WAY TO DO THAT WAS TO **LEAD.**

BUT MORE IMPORTANTLY, I WANTED TO **BE SOMEONE WORTH FOLLOWING.**

For me, it's about striving to be better and sharing that goodness with the world. Benjamin Hardy recently said to me, "The world gives to the givers and takes from the takers." **I want to be one of the givers. I want to inspire those around me.** I firmly believe that's what started this leadership journey for me. I have an insatiable curiosity: I've always wanted to know how to do things better, to learn whatever I can and to grow.

LEADERSHIP, TO ME, IS FOR PEOPLE INTERESTED IN BECOMING BETTER, SHOWING THE WAY AND TEACHING OTHERS TO COME ALONGSIDE THEM TO DO THE SAME.

I THINK THIS BOOK WILL HELP. I AM EXCITED ABOUT GROWING ALONGSIDE YOU. I want to share everything I've learned in my leadership journey over the last 25 years. Through my many managers, coaches and friendships, I've been inspired to find different, better ways.

I've also made sure to surround myself with others who seek leadership greatness. Jon Gordon, the author of *The Power of Positive Leadership* and Seth Godin, who makes you think differently; Kevin Hall, the author of *Aspire*; Darren Hardy, Arianna Huffington, Tony Robbins, Kat Cole,

Andy Stanley, John Maxwell and Brian Tracy. These people—their books, webinars and conferences—all are traveling with me on this journey.

I was on the hunt for better leaders to follow, to emulate and to help push me. But at the end of the day, it came down to one key element.

I had to go first. I had to lead myself. I had to take 100 percent responsibility for my life, my decisions, my direction. I had to quit waiting for someone to lead me, to inspire me or to push me.

I came up with a simple rule that has guided my life ever since...

You Go

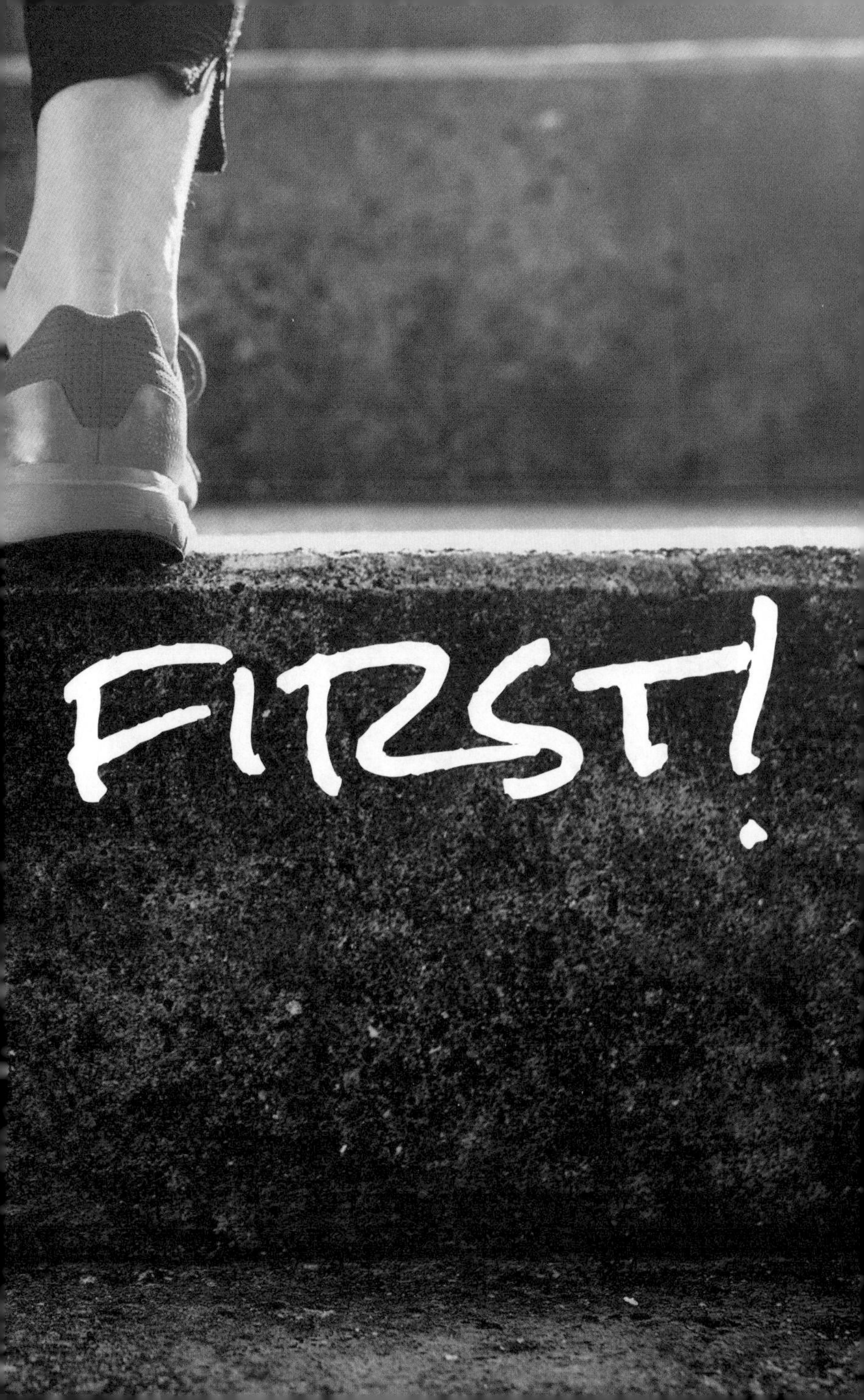
FIRST!

STOP WAITING FOR EVERYONE ELSE AROUND YOU TO STEP UP, WAITING FOR *THINGS* TO GET BETTER.

THINGS **DON'T GET BETTER.** **<u>YOU</u> GET BETTER.**

That one simple rule changed my life in every position and every company I have worked for over the last 30 years. I have worked my way up from the bottom to the top of companies. No matter the company, the position, the duties or my skill set. I made sure I went first. I made sure to have the best attitude, to work the hardest, to do more than was asked, to help others. I was constantly learning and growing. My goal when starting with a new company was to start at the bottom. I wanted to be the last man on the totem pole. **Yes, please.** Let me show you how hard I could work, how I could help, how I would be the first on your radar to move up.

I have held numerous leadership roles with some amazing companies. I have led hundreds of people over the years. It's been a blessing. I am beyond excited to share with you what I have learned along the way. I am still learning. I am far from done. I love that you are still learning and growing with me.

THANKS FOR GOING FIRST BY PICKING UP MY BOOK ON LEADERSHIP. WE NEED YOU.

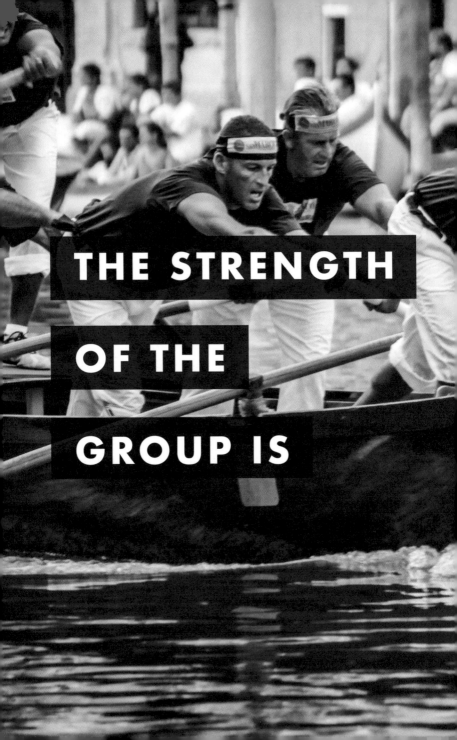

THE STRENGTH
OF THE
GROUP IS

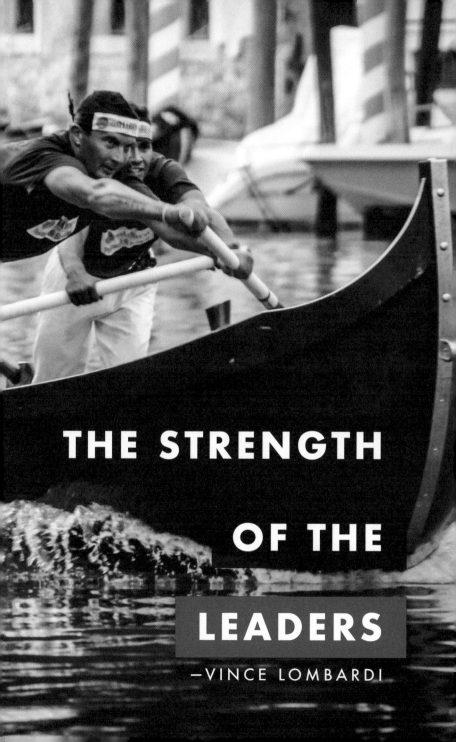

THE STRENGTH

OF THE

LEADERS

—VINCE LOMBARDI

CHAPTER 1

BE THE LEADER YOU WISH YOU HAD

You know the one I'm talking about.

Leaders are everywhere. In your home, in your family, on the playground, in your school, in your workplace, in coffee shops, in the stores you frequent and in our government.

Think about the ones you've had—you know, the *really* good ones.

They cared. They listened. They respected you. They trusted you. They believed in you. They pushed you. They inspired you. They encouraged you. They shared the glory.

Let's be honest...they loved you.

I **loved** all the leaders in my life. I needed them all. The good ones showed me the way. The less-than-stellar ones made me understand that I should never act in that fashion. The gifted ones gave me something to aspire to. Something to hope for. They were someone I wanted to follow.

ARE YOU SOMEBODY WORTH FOLLOWING?

DO YOU WANT TO BE?

BECOMING AN INSPIRING LEADER IS A FULL-TIME JOB AND I AM FAR FROM DONE. BUT MY MISSION IS TO DO JUST THAT: TO BE A BETTER HUMAN, A BETTER LEADER. IT'S ALL ABOUT STRIVING TOWARD GOODNESS AND THEN SHARING THAT WITH THE WORLD.

Each night I thank the stars that I get to spend my days as the Vice President of CBH Homes, the No. 1 homebuilder in the state of Idaho for the past 15 years. I own a real estate company, I'm an award winning author of two books: *Better Human: It's a Full-Time Job* and *Better Thinking: Think Better. Be Better*, and owner of a recently launched company (MORE LIKE A MOVEMENT) called **Better Human.**

I am the poster child for the kid that should have ended up in a roadside ditch. My life from the ages of 3-17 was a first class shit show. I learned from an early age that it was all on me.

I had to lead my life if I was going to make it out alive.

I WAS FORCED TO
BECOME A LEADER.
NO CHOICE ABOUT IT.

Ronda Conger
age 3

But those lessons served me well. I have been in leadership roles for the past 20 years and I'm excited to share with you some of the things I have learned along the way.

I am a mother of two amazing sons and, for the past 26 years, wife to a man I love and respect.

I've been a high school tennis coach and a president of a state youth hockey organization, I've chaired national nonprofit events and I sit on numerous boards in my community.

I'M A LEADER.

IT'S A FULL-TIME JOB.

I AM JUST LIKE YOU.

So glad you are here, so glad you have picked up this book and that you are on the hunt to be a better leader with me. Every morning when the Blue Angels meet, they start their meeting by turning to the guy to their left and the guy to their right and saying, **"So glad you are here."**

And, to you I say, **I AM SO GLAD YOU ARE HERE WITH ME.**

What if you said that very sentence to your spouse, your kids, your roommate or when you rolled into the office each morning? At some point today, turn to someone in your life and let them know you are so glad they are here.

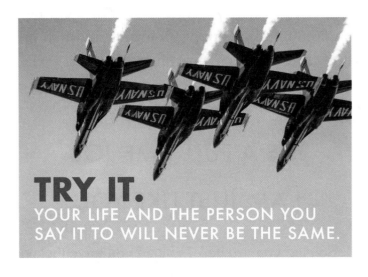

TRY IT.
YOUR LIFE AND THE PERSON YOU SAY IT TO WILL NEVER BE THE SAME.

In one of my last **"Be a Leader of Leaders"** presentations to 50 industry leaders, I asked them to name three things they loved about a past leader.

Here's what they had to say:

THEY CARED ABOUT ME

THEY LED BY EXAMPLE

THEY MADE
EVERYONE BETTER

THEY WERE POSITIVE

THEY WERE CONSISTENT

THEY WERE A GOOD LISTENER

THEY WERE A GO-GETTER

THEY MOTIVATED ME

THEY WERE STRONG IN THEIR
LEADERSHIP SKILLS

THEY WALKED THE TALK

THEY WERE ENTHUSIASTIC

THEY WERE PASSIONATE

THEY SET A GOOD EXAMPLE

You are going to have to stretch out for this journey we are about to embark on together. **You must be all in.** I want a pencil in hand, a highlighter (one with flags, preferably), and sticky notes. We've got some work to do.

Calm down...THE FONT IS LARGE. I've included big pictures, bright colors and some cuss words to keep you engaged. Some people would refer to this book as an airplane book. You can read it on a one- or two-hopper flight and be done. Now, let's get to work.

NAME THREE THINGS YOU LOVED ABOUT A PAST LEADER IN YOUR LIFE. GO.

1.

2.

3.

We could stop the book here and I would just tell you to do those things you listed. It would be one hell of a start.

AFTER PEOPLE TELL ME ABOUT THE THINGS THEY LOVED FROM PAST LEADERS, I THEN ASK, *ARE YOU CURRENTLY DOING ANY OF THOSE ITEMS?*

My favorite replies are *kinda* and *it's hard*. Hence why we can't stop now. Now, consider these:

NAME THREE THINGS YOU DID NOT ENJOY ABOUT ANY OF YOUR PAST LEADERS.

1.

2.

3.

For fun, jump over to Google and search:

Google

| Traits of Terrible Leaders or Bosses 🎤 |

The list is long. Here are some of the worst:

DISMISSING IDEAS
OTHER THAN
YOUR OWN

EGO

BEING TOO SLOW TO ADAPT

POOR COMMUNICATION
OF STRATEGY

ASSIGNING BLAME

TO READ THE COMPLETE LIST
DOWNLOADS.YOUGOFIRST.COM

REPEAT AFTER ME.

DON'T BE THAT GUY.

DO A LEADERSHIP AUDIT. *DAILY.*

DAILY LEADERSHIP AUDIT

☐ Did I hold myself in a professional manner?

....

....

☐ Am I worth following?

....

....

☐ How's my attitude?

....

....

☐ How's my energy level?

....

....

☐ Did I work hard?

....

....

☐ Did I set the pace?

....

....

SUCH POWERFUL QUESTIONS.

The leadership style and attributes of most leaders come from the example set by other leaders (both good and bad) or from the style exhibited by their parents or by simply studying/learning leadership. **To be your own leader and to become a good one, you need to find your own style.** One that helps you become the leader you wish you had. By the end of this book, you may have succeeded in doing just that.

It's GONNA BE FUN.

LET'S GO

TAKE ACTION TO BE BETTER.

YOU GO FIRST.

1.

TELL EVERYONE IN YOUR OFFICE,
ON YOUR VENDOR LIST OR YOUR
PARTNER LIST, AND YOUR FAMILY AND
FRIENDS: *SO GLAD YOU'RE HERE.*

2.

GOOGLE TRAITS OF A TERRIBLE
LEADER. CIRCLE ANY OF THE
TRAITS YOU CURRENTLY EMBODY.
THEN STOP THEM. **IMMEDIATELY.**

3.

DOWNLOAD AND PRINT THE DAILY
LEADERSHIP AUDIT HANDOUT.
PUT IT ON YOUR DESK, YOUR
COMPUTER AND YOUR MIRROR.
THEN SHARE WITH OTHER LEADERS.

CHAPTER 2

ONE SIMPLE RULE

Did you think I was going to jump in and start telling you how to lead other people? What fun is that? You don't get to lead other people until you have learned how to lead yourself. Until you have learned how to run your own damn ranch high and tight.

You go first.

We must learn how to lead ourselves long before we can lead anyone else.

One of my team members came to me and asked the magical question, "How do I become a manager?" Knowing this teammate struggled with being on time, hitting her goals, succumbing to negativity and an unwillingness to serve others, I had to be honest with her. "How can I have you lead other people when you can't seem to lead yourself?" I asked.

FOUR EASY WAYS TO DECIDE WHETHER OR NOT YOU OR SOMEONE AROUND YOU IS READY TO LEAD ARE TO EXAMINE THEIR ATTITUDE, ACTIONS, RESULTS AND CONSISTENCY.

ATTITUDE

Is your attitude amazing? No matter the situation?
Are others excited to be around you?
Do you manage stress or does stress manage you?
Are you a positive person?

ACTIONS

Are your actions worth following?
Do they inspire greatness?
Do you work hard? Or hardly work?
Are you on time? Do you look like a million bucks?

RESULTS

How are your results?
Do you do what is asked of you? Do you do more?
Do you deliver amazing results some of the time...
or all of the time?
Do you inspire greatness?

CONSISTENCY

Are you a one-hit wonder?
Can you lead, day in and day out?

Most people can do some of these things every once in a while. True leaders know there are no days off.

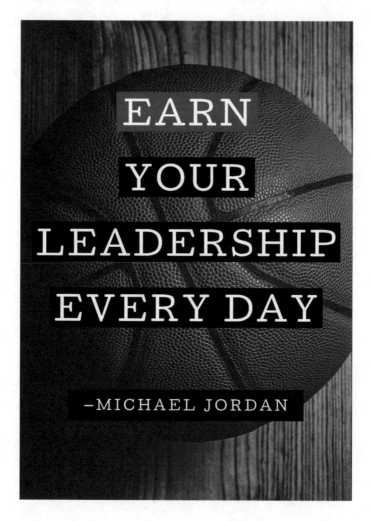

EARN YOUR LEADERSHIP EVERY DAY

–MICHAEL JORDAN

YOU
ARE THE
COMPASS.

Your team is looking to you to decide how they are going to act and work. You set the pace. Your attitude determines their attitude. Your expectations determine what kind of work they will produce. High expectations generally mean your team will put in the work necessary to meet your expectations.

Which direction are you heading?

Do you realize that your ENERGY introduces you before you even speak?

I recently learned of a story about one of my past managers. Her team knew what kind of day it was going to be based on the way she opened the office door and the sound of her shoes as she walked in. The hard, loud and quick walk meant it was going to be a hell of a day. She was going to be angry, short, slightly abusive and fear instilling. If she walked in light as a feather, at a slow gate, then life was good.

Recently, I visited a favorite restaurant of mine. I had heard they were under new ownership and management, so was hopeful the new ownership would be as good, or better, than the last. **It's amazing what you learn when you pay attention.**

My hopes went unrealized that day. Every single employee was rude, short and annoyed with their customers and other servers. They slammed down plates, threw silverware on the table, offered curt replies and did so without a single pleasantry. I then scanned the restaurant for the manager on duty. Easily found her. I watched her body language, interaction with customers and her team. Her team was literally mimicking her. Every action and attitude.

A LEADER SETS THE TONE FOR GOOD—OR BAD.

This happens around us, all of the time. When you are in line at the store, at a coffee shop or at a restaurant, and the person helping you looks and sounds a lot like Darth Vader, they are setting the tone. They are choosing their style of leadership.

Have you ever visited a Dutch Bros. Coffee? You should. Their culture and vibe are worth following. They are happy, eager to serve and flat put it down. The cars and cars of people waiting in line each day go there for caffeine, of course, but they leave with a whole other kind of energy...one gleaned from the happy, responsive team. **The Dutch Bros. company creed says:**

To be so **STRONG** that nothing can disturb your peace of mind. To be just as **ENTHUSIASTIC** about the success of others as you are about your own. To be too **HAPPY** to permit the presence of trouble.

TO READ THE COMPLETE CREED VISIT
DOWNLOADS.YOUGOFIRST.COM

Their owners and leadership team have chosen their attitude.

You choose your attitude in every instance. You choose whether or not you are worth following.

Let's make sure you are mentally strong by keeping in mind these 17 must-dos for leaders:

1. They move on. **They don't waste time feeling sorry for themselves.**

2. They keep control. **They don't give away their power.**

3. They embrace change. **They welcome challenges.**

4. They stay happy. **They don't complain. They don't waste energy on things they can't control.**

5. They are kind, fair and unafraid to speak up. **They don't worry about pleasing other people.**

6. They are willing to take calculated risks. **They weigh the risks and benefits before taking action.**

7. They invest their energy in the present. **They don't dwell on the past.**

8. They accept full responsibility **for their past behavior. They don't make the same mistake over and over.**

9. They celebrate other people's successes. **They don't resent that success.**

10. They are willing to fail. **They don't give up after failing. They see every failure as a chance to improve.**

11. They enjoy their time alone. **They don't fear being alone.**

12. They are prepared to work and succeed on their own merits. **They don't feel the world owes them anything.**

13. They have staying power. **They don't expect immediate results.**

14. They evaluate **their core beliefs and modify as needed.**

15. They expend their mental energy wisely. **They don't spend time on unproductive thoughts.**

16. They think productively. **They replace negative thoughts with productive thoughts.**

17. They tolerate discomfort. **They accept their feelings without being controlled by them.**

Courtesy of Siddharth Talwar

Let's talk about actions. People are watching your actions long before they ever listen to anything you say. A friend of my father's used to say to me, "*Ronda, do as I say, not as I do.*" Keep in mind her actions were less than stellar. I guess I should be grateful that she knew I should NOT follow her actions in any way, shape or form.

It doesn't work that way, folks. You can talk at them all you like, but it's your actions that truly matter. All we are doing is WATCHING YOU. Watching your actions all day, every day.

Is that good news?

If I hung out with you all day today, would your actions inspire me? Excite me? Motivate me? You can watch the sidelines of any NFL professional football game and you don't need a headset to know what that coach is saying to his players.

Just watch his actions. Just watch the yelling, the red face, the spittle flying from his mouth, his clipboard flying through the air. No need for a mic. We know what he's saying.

I am a huge fan of Pete Carroll. Google "NFL Sidelines with Pete Carroll and the Seahawks." You will see him hugging, high fiving, tail slapping and mouthing the words **"I love you, man"** to all of his players throughout the entire game.

Results (aka proof) are in the pudding.

I love to win. I do. I am a firm believer in a scoreboard for all areas of your life. You need to know if you're winning and so does your team.

I'll never forget the simple power of this question:

ARE WE WINNING? ARE WE LOSING?

My family was at the 2007 Tostitos Fiesta Bowl college football bowl game where the Boise State Broncos took on the Oklahoma Sooners in Glendale, Arizona. Boise State was down and all of the Boise State fans, including my family, were sitting on the edge of their seats with the fear of losing looming over us. There were 18 seconds left in the game for us to turn things around. Boise State called a trick play, the Statue of Liberty, and we scored. My entire family and the entire Boise State fan section flew to their feet. We were jumping up and down, yelling and screaming with joy.

I looked down and my 5-year-old son was about knee high, pulling frantically back and forth on my jeans and yelling at me.

"ARE WE WINNING? ARE WE LOSING?" he shouted.

That moment has stuck with me. That's all we want to know. Are we winning with our attitudes? With our actions? With our life?

WALK AROUND. ASK THE PEOPLE IN YOUR LIFE. ARE WE WINNING? ARE WE LOSING? WHAT'S THE SCORE?

Doing the same thing over and over without asking, auditing, inspecting and checking the score is the definition of insanity.

Dwayne "The Rock" Johnson gets consistency.

"SUCCESS ISN'T ALWAYS ABOUT GREATNESS. IT'S ABOUT CONSISTENCY. CONSISTENT, HARD WORK LEADS TO SUCCESS. GREATNESS WILL COME."

—DWAYNE "THE ROCK" JOHNSON

Success isn't always about greatness. It's about consistency. It's about showing up every day. Day in. Day out.

There are no days off when you are a leader.

Show up. Every day.

One of my favorite websites and daily subscriptions is to Hugh MacLeod, GapingVoid.com. He brings to life leadership, work and life with art. Look up his piece titled *How to be Successful*, which he drew for Seth Godin, someone who knows a bit about showing up. You have to show up on Monday, on Tuesday, on Wednesday, on Thursday, on Friday, on Saturday and on Sunday.

Woody Allen once said,

"NINETY PERCENT OF SUCCESS IS JUST SHOWING UP."

It's damn good advice.

I love the story about Jerry Seinfeld and the app he created to make sure he was successful and consistent. It's called *Momentum*. He knew if he could write every day and create consistent content, he would be successful. His daily writing earned him one of the top-grossing television shows of all time. People have been trying to follow his lead and his success ever since.

Bruce Lee is famous for the quote,

"As you think, so shall you become..."

LEADERS GO FIRST. They keep their thoughts clean. Their attitude positive. Their actions inspiring and, most importantly, they deliver results.

LET'S GO

TAKE ACTION TO BE BETTER.

YOU GO FIRST.

1.

WATCH "THE NFL SIDELINES WITH
PETE CARROLL." LOOK UP OTHER
NFL COACHES YOU ADMIRE AND
WATCH THEIR GAME FILMS.

2.

VISIT **GAPINGVOID.COM**
AND FIND THE POST ON
HOW TO BE SUCCESSFUL.

3.

DOWNLOAD THE *MOMENTUM* APP.
LOAD LEADERSHIP HABITS AND THEN
TRACK YOUR SUCCESS.
(Here are a few ideas for habits to load:
tell one person thank you every day, walk
around and praise others, start your
day with "so glad you're here.")

CHAPTER 3

PEER ELEVATION

Who you surround yourself with is one of the biggest decisions you make as a person and as a leader.

One of my favorite quotes is Tony Robbins'

"Proximity is power."

Those you spend time with or who are closest to you will help mold you as a person and determine your level of success. When you are young, it starts with the kids in your neighborhood who become your friends by default. Same thing with school.

A study showed that even when you're a grown adult in college, you still end up being friends with the people that sit the closest to you in class, **not those people who exhibit the most potential, best attitude, positive actions or strong ethics.**

The study also showed that your wealth and your success level oftentimes are based on your zip code. The author states one of the most important things you can do for your kids' future is to change zip codes.

TO READ THE COMPLETE STUDY

DOWNLOADS.YOUGOFIRST.COM

I remember watching a documentary on the Bronx Projects in New York. The residents were on government assistance, on drugs, poor, impoverished and surrounded by gang violence. They said they couldn't get out: "No one makes it out. We are all the same."

BUT I THINK WE ARE BIGGER THAN THAT. TAKE A STEP. LEAVE. MOVE. DO ANYTHING BUT STAY. SURROUND YOURSELF WITH DIFFERENT PEOPLE, DIFFERENT ACTIONS.

JUST GET OUT.

BE ON THE HUNT FOR PEERS AND OPPORTUNITIES THAT ELEVATE YOU. THAT PUSH YOU TO ANOTHER LEVEL. YOU WANT PEOPLE WHO ARE AMBITIOUS.

PEOPLE WHO
ARE HUNGRY.
WHO ARE FULL
OF POTENTIAL.
COACHABLE.
LOVE GROWTH.
LOVE CHANGE.
WHO READ.
WHO DO.
THEY SAY YES.
THEY
ARE DREAMERS.

When we hire new team members, we put them through the gauntlet. We want to make sure they are going in the same direction as we are. That they are moving forward.

One of my favorite tests is **Strengths Finder 2.0** by Tom Rath.

It is a quick online test that helps to define the five things that drive you. Here are my results:

I want to be the **best**. I want to make the most of an **opportunity**. I want to make it **rain**. I will **make things happen.** I will not wait. And I will study, learn and make sure I make the best decisions possible.

TO TAKE THE STRENGTHS FINDER TEST VISIT

DOWNLOADS.YOUGOFIRST.COM

OR GALLUPSTRENGTHSCENTER.COM

Then have your children, your spouse, your team and anyone else you hang with on a regular basis take the test and share it.

Even if I ended up not hiring the person, several of them over the years emailed me and thanked me for the test. It helped them make sure they were on the right path and headed in the right direction.

I will hire someone who is **hungry, positive** and **ready to work** far sooner than someone who is talented but *uncoachable.* One of my favorite books is called *Talent is Overrated* by Geoffrey Colvin. How does that quote go?

"HARD WORK BEATS TALENT WHEN TALENT DOESN'T WORK HARD."

Here are **10 THINGS THAT REQUIRE ZERO TALENT.** Watch for these 10 things when you are hiring (and every day from your team).

10 THINGS
THAT REQUIRE
ZERO TALENT

1. Being on Time
2. Work Ethic
3. Effort
4. Body Language
5. Energy
6. Attitude
7. Passion
8. Being Coachable
9. Doing Extra
10. Being Prepared

DOWNLOAD & SHARE THIS HANDOUT
DOWNLOADS.YOUGOFIRST.COM

Now, for the million-dollar question,

"What do you do if you don't have the right team members or the right people around you?"

The answer is simple.

CLEAN HOUSE.

Time to sit down with the person and talk it out. You might love the person, just not their behaviors.

Can they change their behaviors? Can they do what it's going to take to be on your team? If yes, ask them to stay. If not, let them go so they are freed up for a different opportunity.

LET GO TO GO UP.

Let go of the people, the attitudes, the actions that do not serve you as you strive to achieve your goals.

Your job as a leader is not only to surround yourself with the best, but also to ensure you are doing everything possible to move forward.

ALWAYS GOING UP.

Fifteen years ago when I started working at CBH Homes, I inherited someone else's team. That can be rough because you are TAKING ON SOMEONE ELSE'S TEAM. That team was chosen because of what was important to the past leader. They all held the same attitudes, actions and work ethic as the past leader.

And it *was* rough, at first. But then I sat down with each team member and defined my style of leadership. I was clear that my expectations would be high. Those first six months were brutal. I almost could hear the song, "Another One Bites the Dust" coming out of the walls. Every single day someone would come into my office singing the same tune: the expectations were too high, they were working too hard, I was being unrealistic. When all was said and done, we ended up replacing almost 90 percent of the team. My hope going in was that they would stay; that they would drink the Kool-Aid. Don't get me wrong, I really liked quite a few of them. **They just weren't a good fit for where I wanted to take the team and company going forward.**

So. You have cleaned house, you have
hired smart and now you have the best team.

NOW WHAT?

Your job as the leader is to encourage
your team to work in their areas
of strength, to shine, to thrive.

Your job as the leader is to share
new books, give access to different
classes, blogs and podcasts throughout
the year. Keep elevating your team.

Bring them with you. One of my all-time favorite leadership conferences each year is **Leadercast.** They bring together the most diverse and inspiring leaders in the nation. I ask my crew to fill out a growth plan form every year. At the end of that period, the person with the most growth items wins a trip to Leadercast Live in Atlanta.

For all of us, the conference is unforgettable. Who wouldn't like to be encouraged by the likes of:

MAYOR RUDY GIULIANI

PEYTON MANNING

NICK SABAN

COACH K *(MIKE KRZYZEWSKI)*

SETH GODIN

KAT COLE

JOHN MAXWELL

MOLLY FLETCHER

RORKE DENVER

OR

ANDY STANLEY?

Put Leadercast on your leadership
bucket list. It will be worth it.

LEADERCAST.COM/PAGES/LIVE

LET'S GO

TAKE ACTION TO BE BETTER.

YOU GO FIRST.

1.

TAKE THE STRENGTHS FINDER
TEST. THEN HAVE YOUR TEAM
AND FAMILY TAKE IT.

2.

GO TO DOWNLOADS.YOUGOFIRST.COM
TO READ THE "PROXIMITY
IS POWER" ARTICLE.

3.

DO AN AUDIT OF THE PEOPLE
CLOSEST TO YOU.

LET GO
TO GO
UP

CHAPTER 4

PASSIONATE AND CAFFEINATED

I look for two things:

I WANT YOU PASSIONATE & CAFFEINATED.

Passionate about yourself, about your potential, about your life, about your work, about your career, about your marriage, about your kids, about your friends.

NOTHING ELSE WILL DO.

We have come up with this new rule that says when someone asks you to do something, it better evoke a **HELL, YES** out of you. If it doesn't, then you shouldn't do it. Don't go through life just kinda happy, kinda liking something.

When you commit to things in your life, you should not hear the following statements...

sure, yup, why not, who cares,

nothing better, I guess.

You get it. I am looking for the **HELL, YES** type of people.

My husband likes to tell people that I'm a full tank of gas.

Caffeinated is my version of having a big engine. Someone who always answers the call.

THE DOER.

A PERSON WHO FLAT PUTS IT DOWN.

THE HUSTLER.

THE RAINMAKER.

THE NINJA.

> **YOU SEE, ANYONE CAN BE TRAINED ON HOW TO USE A SOFTWARE SYSTEM OR A PROCESS, OR LEARN A PRODUCT LINE.**
>
> **WHAT I CAN'T TEACH YOU IS HOW TO BE PASSIONATE AND CAFFEINATED.**

Search these types of people out.

Work on becoming one of these people if you are a leader.

One of the leaders in my company recently asked if I could make a Ronda Conger doll with a string that you could pull to dispense energy, motivation and inspiration as needed.

I've learned that most people appreciate and covet my energy.

You can have it, too. You can. But it takes intention. It can't just happen. In fact, each day I am known to do these five things to fill my own energy tank. They will work for you, too:

1. BE THANKFUL FOR EVERY BREATH.
   **I AM LITERALLY BLOWN AWAY BY
   EVERY SECOND I GET ON THIS EARTH.
   BEING THANKFUL GETS ME PRETTY
   FIRED UP.**

2. I LOVE THE OPPORTUNITY TO BUILD
   DREAMS FOR THOUSANDS UPON
   THOUSANDS OF HOMEBUYERS.
   PLAINLY STATED, I ADORE MY CAREER.

3. I WORK ON MY LIFE.
   I'M EXCITED FOR MY POTENTIAL.

4. I'M ON A MISSION TO
   BE BETTER EVERY DAY.

5. I LOVE ALL THOSE I COME IN
   CONTACT WITH. **I DO. I LOVE THEM
   FOR THE LESSONS, FOR THE JOY, FOR
   THE KINDNESS, FOR THE FUN, FOR
   THE EXAMPLE.**

BUT NONE OF THESE WORK UNLESS YOU KNOW YOUR OWN "WHY." WHY DO YOU WANT TO BE A GOOD LEADER? WHY DO YOU WANT THE THINGS YOU WANT?

The movie *Cinderella Man* is one of my favorites. Russell Crowe is a down-on-his-luck fighter and comes back to win it all with fury, energy and passion.

They asked him how he did it, what he was fighting for.

His answer was milk.

Earlier in the movie he lost it all. Money, home, food and his job were all gone for him, his children and wife. He promised himself that if he ever got the chance to fight again, he wouldn't forget what he was fighting for. He wouldn't take it for granted. He would do better.

Milk represented his ability to take care of his family.

What's going to get you up before your alarm clock? What's going to get you to be the first one to work or the last one to leave?

SHARE YOUR PASSION AND YOUR WHY WITH YOUR TEAM.

The why comes in all kinds of different shapes and sizes. Here's a list of whys to help you understand why people do what they do:

They love what the company does. For example, we are a home-building company. I love that we build people's dreams.

They love the particular skill they have been hired for. One of my teammates LOVES spreadsheets. She is over the moon when she gets to create magic with numbers.

They love the idea of working with a team.

They love helping customers; they love to serve.

They have a bucket list that is full and they need to finance their dreams.

They want to be part of something successful.

They have a best friend at work and want to hang out with them.

FIND OUT THEIR WHY AND THEN
GET BUSY FIGHTING FOR IT.

Want to know my why? What gets me out of bed?

I want another shot to be better. To give as much love as possible. I want to be better and share it with the world while building people's dreams. I want my actions, attitude and energy to inspire others. My bucket list is long. My dreams are BIG. World domination seems completely doable to me.

Some people think I shotgun Red Bull daily. No need.

I AM PASSIONATE AND HAVE A VERY BIG ENGINE FOR THIS THING CALLED LIFE.

If you need some energy, call the Red Bull crew. Did you know that the Red Crew will come to your office and hand out Red Bulls to your entire office for free?!? WHAT?!? We have them come to company meetings and random days throughout the year to fill our teams' tanks. Do it. They are amazing.

A national study was conducted on what separated winning and losing teams in the NBA. They wanted to see something other than free throw percentages, three pointers, fouls, etc.

INSTEAD, THEY COUNTED THE NUMBER OF TIMES A TEAM HIGH FIVED, BRO HUGGED, FIST BUMPED AND SO ON. THE STUDY REVEALED THAT TEAMS WITH PLAYERS WHO WERE PASSIONATE ABOUT THEIR TEAMMATES AND THE GAME IN GENERAL HAD MORE TOUCHES LIKE THE ABOVE REFERENCED THAN ANY OTHER TEAM.

**THEY PROVED THAT BY SHARING
THEIR ENTHUSIASM, IT LED TO
MORE CONFIDENCE, MORE LOVE,
MORE ENERGY, MORE PASSION
FOR THE GAME, MORE WINS AND
MORE BELIEF. IT REDUCED ANXIETY
AND REDUCED THEIR FEARS.**

READ THE COMPLETE STUDY AT

DOWNLOADS.YOUGOFIRST.COM

How does this translate into something you can actually do as a leader?

Walk around more, reach out more, FaceTime, call or email, send a text, high five your team every time you walk by them. Get crazy and throw in a hug. **Just make a connection.** Your team needs it (craves it); your family needs it (craves it). Jon Gordon, author and speaker, says you have two choices when you come in contact with him: **fist pump or hug. Your choice.**

Speaking of family, we have a hard rule in my house that whenever you see a family member upon entering our home, a restaurant or an event you must hug them. You must make contact.

SEEK OUT THE
PASSIONATE AND
THE BIG ENGINES.

AND REMEMBER:
YOU GO FIRST.

LET'S GO

TAKE ACTION TO BE BETTER.

YOU GO FIRST.

1.

WATCH *CINDERELLA MAN.*

2.

MAKE CONTACT WITH YOUR
TEAM, YOUR FAMILY. TRY IT.

3.

DEFINE YOUR WHY. THEN ASK
YOUR TEAMMATES THEIR WHY.

CHAPTER 5

WHAT'S FUN GOT TO DO WITH IT? EVERYTHING

Tell your friends. Tell your team. Tell the world.

WORK IS

YOU SPEND TOO MUCH TIME AT WORK FOR IT NOT TO BE FUN!

MY COMPANY, CBH HOMES, WAS VOTED THE BEST PLACE TO WORK IN IDAHO THIS YEAR. OF COURSE WE WERE. P.S. THIS IS AN OUTSIDE SURVEY VOTED ON BY THE EMPLOYEES! WE ARE A FLAT GOOD TIME. WHAT DOES THAT LOOK LIKE?

HAPPY HOURS
YOGA CASINO NIGHTS
FLASH MOBS
TAILGATE PARTIES
SILLY STRING WARS
COFFEE RUNS
BIRTHDAY CELEBRATIONS
NERF GUN WARS
BOOK CLUBS
PANCAKE FEEDS
CASH GIVEAWAYS
SCARING COMPETITIONS
MUSIC VIDEOS
AMAZING RACE CONTESTS
TACO TUESDAYS
COMPANY MOVIES DURING THE DAY
DANCE PARTIES
TEAM BONDING HIKES
LIP-SYNC BATTLES
OFF-THE-HOOK CHRISTMAS PARTIES
PHOTO BOOTHS

I recently heard a college football coach discuss the reason his team was losing. He said that it started with him. He had made the locker room full of tension and anxiety.

Fun had left the building.

He pulled his team together to remind them they were forgetting the key ingredient to their success. They were forgetting the fun.

Is that you? Have you forgotten that we need to enjoy our days?

WE NEED TO HAVE FUN WHILE WE PRODUCE GREAT THINGS.

Don't be the buzz kill.

Don't be the party pooper. Tara, my personal cheerleader, has a song she will totally sing to you if you truly are that guy. It goes something like "every party needs a pooper...that's why we invited you."

When I started with CBH Homes 15 years ago, the owner, Corey Barton, and I promised each other the #1 thing we would do together is have **fun.**

I love when people ask me if I am still with CBH Homes. Of course I am! I am having way too much fun with an amazing group of people.

People don't hang around very long if they are not having fun. We are wired for fun. It started at birth. It's a thing.

We all need it.

DO A FUN AUDIT. IF YOU AREN'T THE FUN-BOBBY TYPE, THEN DELEGATE IT OUT. IT'S THAT IMPORTANT.

WALK THROUGH YOUR OFFICE.

DO PEOPLE LOOK HAPPY, ENGAGED, PASSIONATE?

Be on the hunt for companies or teams you want to emulate. We toured Zappos years ago after Tony Hsieh released his book. I had to see behind the curtain.

If you haven't toured their office, you should. It's in Las Vegas. I highly recommend the Zappos Chow & WOW Tour Experience. Per square inch, it's the most fun you can have. I could go on for days about what I learned and saw. Tailgate parties inside the office, ball pit for adults, Captain Crunch cereal dispensers, putting ranges, remote control cars, ping-pong, skateboards and so much more.

Last year, TSheets, a local company on its way to world domination, won the #1 spot for best places to work. We called them immediately and asked for a tour. We learned so much. They literally give employees a Pabst Blue Ribbon beer on their first day. It's true! They call it "THE PBR Core Values." Go look it up on their website! We are crushing all over them and picked up a few new ideas to make us better and to make us more FUN.

Be a student of fun. It pays to have fun.

LIST THREE COMPANIES YOU ADMIRE AND WANT TO BE LIKE:

1.

2.

3.

NOW CALL THEM AND SET UP A TOUR. *MIC DROP.*

In the Monster.com article "Why Having Fun at Work Matters," the authors Adrian Gostick and Scott Christopher noted:

"IF PEOPLE ARE HAVING **FUN**, THEY'RE GOING TO WORK HARDER, STAY LONGER, MAINTAIN THEIR COMPOSURE IN A CRISIS AND TAKE BETTER CARE OF THE ORGANIZATION."

The research showed that when leaders work to create a fun workplace, there is a huge increase in trust, creativity and communication, which in turn helps reduce turnover, increase morale and build a stronger bottom line. The article goes on to show that managers who have taught themselves to be funnier are more effective communicators and better salespeople, have more engaged employees, and even earn a lot more than their peers. It would appear that a big chunk of Fortune's "100 Best Companies to Work For" scores well on the fun question.

READ THE RESEARCH AT

DOWNLOADS.YOUGOFIRST.COM

Spoiler alert...my next book will be all about **CULTURE**. We will be sharing our "love wins" philosophy, what we do, how we do it, how to implement it and to be thought of as one of the best places to work. Break out the blow horns, the tacos, the dance floors and tutus! IT'S GOING TO GET WESTERN.

WHAT'S
GOT TO
LEADER

FUN
DO WITH
SHIP?

EVERY

THING

LET'S GO

TAKE ACTION TO BE BETTER.

YOU GO FIRST.

1.

TOUR ZAPPOS.

2.

DO ONE ITEM FROM MY FUN
LIST. *TACO TUESDAYS ANYONE?*

3.

RESEARCH AND VISIT A COMPANY
YOU ADMIRE IN YOUR AREA.

CHAPTER 6

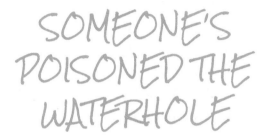

SOMEONE'S POISONED THE WATERHOLE

Have you heard the story about the guy who lost his six-figure income job?

HIS BOSS LISTED THE 50 REASONS HE LOST HIS JOB:

1. HIS ATTITUDE
2. HIS ATTITUDE
3. HIS ATTITUDE
4. HIS ATTITUDE
5. HIS ATTITUDE
6. HIS ATTITUDE
7. HIS ATTITUDE
8. HIS ATTITUDE
9. HIS ATTITUDE
10. HIS ATTITUDE
11. HIS ATTITUDE
12. HIS ATTITUDE
13. HIS ATTITUDE
14. HIS ATTITUDE
15. HIS ATTITUDE
16. HIS ATTITUDE
17. HIS ATTITUDE
18. HIS ATTITUDE
19. HIS ATTITUDE
20. HIS ATTITUDE
21. HIS ATTITUDE
22. HIS ATTITUDE
23. HIS ATTITUDE
24. HIS ATTITUDE
25. HIS ATTITUDE

26. HIS ATTITUDE
27. HIS ATTITUDE
28. HIS ATTITUDE
29. HIS ATTITUDE
30. HIS ATTITUDE
31. HIS ATTITUDE
32. HIS ATTITUDE
33. HIS ATTITUDE
34. HIS ATTITUDE
35. HIS ATTITUDE
36. HIS ATTITUDE
37. HIS ATTITUDE
38. HIS ATTITUDE
39. HIS ATTITUDE
40. HIS ATTITUDE
41. HIS ATTITUDE
42. HIS ATTITUDE
43. HIS ATTITUDE
44. HIS ATTITUDE
45. HIS ATTITUDE
46. HIS ATTITUDE
47. HIS ATTITUDE
48. HIS ATTITUDE
49. HIS ATTITUDE
50. HIS ATTITUDE

HOW'S YOUR ATTITUDE?
HOW'S YOUR
TEAM'S ATTITUDE?
YOU GO FIRST.
HERE'S A SIMPLE RULE
FOR LIFE, FOR YOUR
TEAMS, FOR YOU:
WHEN THE
MOOD IS
POSITIVE
EVERYTHING IS
POSSIBLE.

YES! I would love to work on an extra project.

YES! I would love to come in early.

YES! I would love to stay late.

YES! I would love to sell more.

YES! I would love to help a new team member.

YES! I would love to work this weekend.

YES! I can!

THAT IS WHAT A POSITIVE MOOD LOOKS LIKE.

You see, being negative in a negative situation is easy. Anyone can do it. But that's not you. You are the leader. You must realize that it's your job to solve the issue quickly and move forward. Being negative is like grinding it out in first or second gear. Or worse, like slamming a car into reverse.

You have one direction

and that is FORWARD.

Always forward.

Don't let the naysayers, the negative ones, the pessimists, the glass-half-empty people derail you. Ralph Marston in *The Daily Motivator* says it best:

"BEING POSITIVE IN A NEGATIVE SITUATION IS NOT BEING NAIVE. IT'S CALLED LEADERSHIP."

COMPLAINING
IS A HABIT.

LOSING
IS A HABIT.

HAPPINESS
IS A HABIT.

WINNING
IS A HABIT.

My son and his friends love to play dunk ball. One night, after a hard-fought game of dunk ball, I overheard his friends talking about the game. The losing team was complaining about the fouls, their injuries and all the reasons why they lost. My son's friend on the winning team had this to say: **"It's okay, winning isn't for everyone."**

What's your habit?

Ten years ago I read a book called *The Good Life Rules* by Bryan Dodge and it inspired me to send out a positive thought, quote or an excerpt from a book to my team every day. He assured me that this effort would help to get my head straight and to help my team focus on the right things each day. It's been 10 years since I've started following those guidelines and sending out encouragements. Since then, thousands of people have been added to my email list. My team has asked me to add their spouses, their kids, other family members, friends and business partners.

It turns out we all need a little something to keep us moving in the right direction.

"Someone's poisoned the waterhole" comes from one of my favorite movies. *Toy Story!* You guessed it! Right?

YOUR **"WATERHOLE"** IS YOUR COMPANY, YOUR TEAM, YOUR DEPARTMENT, YOUR FAMILY, YOUR FRIENDS. ARE YOU SURROUNDING YOURSELF WITH POSITIVE, UPLIFTING DOERS? WITH EXCITED, PASSIONATE, CAFFEINATED TYPES OF PEOPLE?

If you already do, then please know that I am cheering for you right now. I am giving you a virtual high five. Keep it up. Focus on the good. Hire the positive.

If you have some work to do, I am going to give you three easy steps:

1. Audit yourself first.
Make sure you are headed
in the right direction
with the right attitude.

2. Audit your team. Is your
team positive, both toward
you or toward your team in
general? Or just you? Ask
other teammates. Dig a little.

3. Meet with anyone that
is not in line with what it
takes to be on your team.

Challenge them to a **RED RUBBER BAND CHALLENGE.** Your whole team wears a red rubber band for a week and every time **ANYONE** complains or is negative, each member of the team has to snap his own band.

This helps to hold the whole team accountable to not allow such behaviors. It also helps the person with the negative mind-set to become aware and stop.

You must be open and honest with the people on your team. Set the expectation and hold it. Offer to help them work on their mindset and move forward. If they can't, then you need to set them free for other opportunities with other companies.

I recently read Michael Hyatt's blog, **The 5 Characteristics of Weak Leaders.** He uses President Lincoln and General George B. McClellan as poignant examples of what not to do:

> Like all of us, Lincoln's leadership was not perfect. He occasionally hired people who were unworthy of his trust...General McClellan [for example] had significant character flaws that I believe serve as warning signs to anyone in leadership. Ultimately, these cost him dearly: He lost Lincoln's confidence, his job and a run for the White House (against Lincoln). Worse, they prolonged the Civil War and cost the lives of tens of thousands of soldiers on both sides of the conflict.

HERE ARE THE FIVE FLAWS I JOTTED DOWN AS I READ THE BLOG.

1. Hesitating to take definitive action.

Are you always preparing but never ready? Remember done is better than perfect. General McClellan could not bring himself to launch an attack. When Lincoln finally relieved him of his duties, he famously said, "If General McClellan does not want to use the army, I would like to borrow it for a time."

2. Complaining about a lack of resources.

McClellan was known for constantly complaining about the lack of available resources. You will never have enough resources. It's your job to make do with what you have been given.

3. Refusing to take responsibility.

McClellan blamed everyone else for his mistakes. He even blamed the big guy. Every time he suffered a defeat or a setback, someone or something was to blame. He was a master. Don't be a finger pointer. Be accountable for the results. Both the good and the bad.

4. Abusing the privileges of leadership. Don't use your power to make your life amazing while your team suffers. You can't make decisions with only yourself in mind.

5. Engaging in acts of insubordination. While the word insubordination refers to someone who is being disobedient or disrespectful, the definition for insubordination is more specific. When insubordination occurs at work, it is more than just being disrespectful, it is the refusal of an employee to take a direct order from a supervisor or it involves a confrontation between an employee and a supervisor. Both of these acts will usually end in severe consequences for the employee.

President Lincoln ended up releasing McClellan. Of course he did.

These same character flaws afflict many leaders today. The best safeguard is self-awareness. **Here's one more simple test for you and your team:**

WHICH
ONE
ARE YOU?

ARE PEOPLE HAPPY TO SEE YOU WHEN YOU WALK INTO THE OFFICE...

OR DO THEY TURN AND NOT MAKE EYE CONTACT?

All we ask is that you don't pollute our day. Please don't share all of your problems, aches, pains, ailments, kid drama, marriage blues or your dog's vet visits. Take this outside of the office. Think about social media. Are you posting that your life sucks on facebook? Yikes! Yes, your team, your family and your 1,000 friends on Facebook will see it and read it. **Don't pollute our day— we beg of you.**

I get it. We all have messy lives. But at work, we need to be on our game. If your team is chatty, have a small (small being the key word) share rule with your team. Share for five minutes upon arrival about your "stuff" with one, maybe two, close friends in the office, and then don't mention it again. Let's get focused on the mission at hand. Let's take a break for the day from your train wreck 101 and revisit it at 5:01 p.m.

Go here and watch this three-minute video. Tony Robbins has it down. He knows how to be a leader worth following.

HEAR TONY IN HIS OWN WORDS AT
DOWNLOADS.YOUGOFIRST.COM

For those of you with no internet handy, here's how to be more attractive *(both as a leader and as a person)* **per Tony Robbins:**

TRADE YOUR EXPECTATIONS FOR APPRECIATION AND YOUR WHOLE LIFE CHANGES.

STOP WHINING.

STOP COMPLAINING.

STOP BEING A BUMMER TO BE AROUND.

BE GENEROUS.

BE LOVING.

BE PLAYFUL.

BE SINCERE.

BE HAPPY.

APPRECIATE YOUR LIFE.

IT'S THAT SIMPLE.

People think you have to choose between positivity and winning. **You don't have to choose. Positivity leads to winning.** That's an excerpt from Jon Gordon's new book, *The Power of Positive Leadership*. It's currently on my nightstand. Can I tell you—I'm in love with it!

*DOG-EAR THIS PAGE, SO YOU CAN BUY HIS BOOK WHEN YOU ARE DONE WITH THIS ONE.

POSITIVITY LEADS TO WINNING.

You Go

FIRST!

LET'S GO

TAKE ACTION TO BE BETTER.

YOU GO FIRST.

1.

AUDIT YOUR ATTITUDE AND YOUR
TEAM'S. ADJUST ACCORDINGLY.

2.

BUY RED RUBBER BANDS AND DO
THE RED RUBBER BAND CHALLENGE.

3.

WATCH TONY ROBBINS' VIDEO.

CHAPTER 7

FEAR IS NOT A STRATEGY

Fear has its place and is something we all have in us. As leaders, though, the thing we should be most fearful of is becoming obsolete, of not making enough progress, the fear of our clients choosing someone else or the fear that we didn't do the work well—or at all.

GOOD LEADERSHIP ELIMINATES THESE FEARS AT THE OUTSET. **STRONG LEADERS OUTLINE WHAT IT TAKES TO BE A PART OF THE TEAM OR COMPANY.**

Those leaders regularly inspect how team members are doing with the expectations. If the team member is unable to meet the demands consistently or regularly disregards your mission, then the decision to part ways has been made, and you say **good-bye.**

We all can agree that reminding someone to get to work or face losing the job seldom works in the long run. Threats only set off wildfires as disgruntled employees share the words of the "unreasonable boss" who expects too much. Fear rarely does the trick.

INSTEAD, FEAR INSTILLS PANIC. FEAR MAKES PEOPLE STOP, QUESTION EVERYTHING, SWING THE PENDULUM AND EVENTUALLY DO NOTHING PRODUCTIVE.

Henry Ford, the famous automaker, was known for saying, **"Your job as leader is to set the table, not clear it."** You want people to join your team, not leave or run from it.

INSTEAD, RELY ON THE SIMPLE PRINCIPLE OF CAUSE & EFFECT:

If you are consistently late or no-showing for work, *you will be asked to leave.*

If you steal, lie or cheat the company, *you will be asked to leave.*

If you fail to do what is required in your position at a mutually agreed upon level, *you will be asked to leave.*

When you hire someone, set up the basic ground rules for their employment with you and create standard operating procedures for every team member. It outlines what the leader expects of them, day in and day out. There is no grey on what success looks like or what is expected of them to keep their job.

After the ground rules are established, review that list carefully. Ask them to do what's on their list every day. Ask them to have an amazing attitude. Ask them to be grateful for the opportunity. Do these things, and you will succeed in the company.

Do this with everyone, including the leaders on your team. Hire only those who will take ownership of their position, their responsibilities.

YOUR JOB AS THE LEADER IS TO REMOVE ROADBLOCKS, GIVE OPPORTUNITIES TO SUCCEED AND ENCOURAGE TEAM MEMBERS TO GROW.

THREATENING, YELLING OR INSTILLING FEAR ARE LOSING HABITS.

WINNING TAKES OPTIMISM, BELIEF, DIRECTION, HOPE AND FAITH.

"Don't even f#$&ing look down here, Conger." This is what one of my son's past coaches said to him as they were losing a game. My son kept looking at the coach (the leader) trying to see what he was going to do to turn things around, how he was going to react, what his direction or guidance might be.

The coach answered with fear. (In case you were wondering, they lost the game.)

Coaches and teams always have intrigued me. How they handle themselves when they are winning and when they are losing. I always start with the leader—I watch him first. What are we seeing in the body language or verbal cues? How are they interacting with their team, regardless of the score?

LOSING BEHAVIORS OF COACHES AND TEAMS:

Coach has arms crossed. He is
pacing, swearing, scowling.
Team is sitting down with their
heads between their legs.
The sideline is relatively quiet.
Occasional outbursts of yelling by coach.

WINNING BEHAVIORS OF COACHES AND TEAMS:

Coach is high fiving, bro-
hugging, slapping tails.
Coach and players are smiling,
laughing, fist pumping.
Players are standing/jumping up and down.
Players are bringing on the Gatorade
bucket over the coach's head.

What I have never understood is that the winning behaviors are the EASIEST ones to have.

Anyone can be a leader when they're winning.

I want to know what you revert to under pressure. You, as a leader, are needed most in high-pressure, stressful situations when you are losing. This is the time when the team is looking to you to decide how they should respond.

Should they be angry?
Fearful?
Sullen?
Quiet?
Reclusive?
Unapproachable?
Defeated?

True leaders understand that when a team is losing, they need their leaders the most. Anyone can high five after someone scores. I want to know if you high five them when they screw up, when they don't score?

Do you tell them you still believe in them and to get back out there?

Or do you threaten them? Try to scare them into better performance?

YOU SEE, THE PROBLEM ISN'T THE PROBLEM. IT'S YOUR ATTITUDE TOWARD THE PROBLEM.

When someone is not winning or succeeding on your team, you need to go first. Answer the following questions:

1. Did you give them enough training?

2. Have you been giving them ongoing training?

3. Did you strive to make them better?

4. Did you give them the tools they need for success?

5. Did you communicate effectively and consistently?

6. Do you believe in them and their abilities?

7. Did you set them up for success or failure?

8. Did you give them the right tools?

Sometimes as leaders we need to realize that we are the ones who failed. Our job is to set our teams up for success.

Show the way. Lead the way. Invite them to join you.

Being positive in a negative situation is not naive. It's called leadership.
—Ralph Marston, The Daily Motivator

When you are struggling, when things are going the wrong direction, when you are straight-up frustrated with someone on your team or your entire team, for that matter, you have to stop and ask yourself:

WOULD MY REACTION HELP OR HURT THE SITUATION?

WOULD IT HELP?

Expect problems and eat them for breakfast. I read an article years ago that mentioned that 85 percent of a leader's day is spent handling problems.

This just in: It's your job to put out fires, handle issues, clear the way and remove roadblocks for your team.

They're not out in front. You are.

Andy Stanley is one of my favorite authors and speakers. I heard him speak at Leadercast in Atlanta a few years back. He talked about one of the greater pieces of advice he had ever received. It was a story about a cage and a 900-pound gorilla.

The story went like this: To be a good leader, you have to open the cage, get in there with the 900-pound gorilla, and solve the issue. That's your job.

Are you willing to open the cage?

Andrea Walker-Leidy, owner of Walker Publicity, says it best: "Leadership is the ability to see a problem and be the solution. So many people are willing to talk about problems or even empathize, but not many can see the problem or challenge and rise to it. It takes a leader to truly see a problem as a challenge and want to drive toward it. That is what causes people to want to follow, and a true leader has a following."

Do you have a following? A team that respects and loves you?

Or is your team fearful and paranoid that at any moment they will be yelled at, or worse, let go?

I literally cringe when I talk to leaders and managers who tell me how easy it is to find their team's errors. News flash! If that's all you're looking for, that's all you'll find. We need to find the wins, emphasize the strengths, and train/manage the errors. No one I know wants to do a crappy job.

FINDING FAULT IS EASY. WE ARE HUMANS. WE ARE MESSY.

THAT'S WHY I SPEND MY TIME LOOKING FOR PASSION, ATTITUDE, EFFORT, CARE, LOVE AND DRIVE.

Try this **Focus Exercise** for the next 30 days. Every day at the end of your day, write 30 wins from your day and 30 wins from your team's performance for the day. You will be amazed at how your perspective changes.

I see leaders get it all wrong. They search out problems, people's faults, all the negatives; everything that's wrong versus all the good. Let's do a focus check-in.

Write down 30 things that come to mind when you think about your team and your day.

Focus on what went right; focus on the people who work hard, clients you love, vendors who make you better:

DOWNLOAD THE FOCUS 30 EXERCISE AT
DOWNLOADS.YOUGOFIRST.COM

1. _____
2. _____
3. _____
4. _____
5. _____
6. _____
7. _____
8. _____
9. _____
10. _____
11. _____
12. _____
13. _____
14. _____
15. _____
16. _____
17. _____
18. _____
19. _____
20. _____
21. _____
22. _____
23. _____
24. _____
25. _____
26. _____
27. _____
28. _____
29. _____
30. _____

I'm looking for the wins. How about you?

Let's do some simple math.

Google gives us these definitions of fear and inspire:

Definition of Fear
fear /'fir/ *noun:*
an unpleasant emotion caused by the belief that someone or something is dangerous, likely to cause pain, or a threat.

Synonyms: terror, fright, fearfulness, horror, alarm, panic, agitation, trepidation, dread, consternation, dismay, distress.

Definition of Inspire
in·spire /in'spī(ə)r/ *verb:*
fill (someone) with the urge or ability to do or feel something

Synonyms: stimulate, motivate, encourage, influence, rouse, move, stir, energize, galvanize, incite.

IS YOUR END GAME TO

BRING *TERROR, ALARM,*

PANIC, DISTRESS OR *DREAD*

TO YOUR TEAM EACH DAY?

OR IS IT TO *MOTIVATE,*

ENCOURAGE, INFLUENCE,

MOVE, ENERGIZE OR *INCITE?*

YOU CHOOSE EVERY DAY.

YOU GO FIRST.

LET'S GO

TAKE ACTION TO BE BETTER.

YOU GO FIRST.

1.

TAKE THE *WOULD-IT-HELP CHALLENGE.*
PICK YOUR LAST REACTION TO
A PROBLEM. DID IT HELP THE
PROBLEM OR MAKE IT WORSE?

2.

DO THE FOCUS 30 CHALLENGE.

3.

INSPIRE OR FEAR. CHOOSE **ONE**.

CHAPTER 8

PEOPLE QUIT. YUP, THEY DO.

People on your team are going to quit.

Yup. They will.

All of the time.

Can we please stop running around chanting:

People don't quit their jobs, they quit their managers.

Yes, SOME people quit because they have crappy managers.

Some leave because...

THEY MOVE.
THEY RETIRE.
THEY WANT A NEW CAREER.
THEY WANT MORE MONEY.
THEY THINK THE GRASS IS GREENER.
THEY CAN'T STAND THEIR CUBICLE.
THEY READ, EAT, PRAY, LOVE.
THE REASONS ARE ENDLESS.

My personal cheerleader has been with me for 18 years minus a brief 1.5 years sabbatical we like to call her Eat, Pray, Love time. She has been by my side since she was 16 years old. She is one of the hardest working, smartest, happiest, most positive people I have ever met. She is a gift. It was crazy HARD to let her go. I knew I had to. I gave her as much love as I could and wished her well. **Spoiler alert...she came back.**

As a leader you can't be selfish. It can't be all about you and what you want. She helped me understand that. Yes, I needed her to stay, but it wasn't about me. I welcomed her back with open arms.

WHEN I AM LEADING PEOPLE, THESE ARE MY HOPES:

I INSPIRE MY TEAM TO STAY AND WORK WITH ME.

I GIVE THEM OPPORTUNITY TO GROW.

I LOVE THEM ACCORDINGLY.

I CHALLENGE THEM.

I TAKE CARE OF THEM.

I HELP THEM IN ALL AREAS OF THEIR LIVES.

I GIVE MORE THAN I TAKE.

I SAY THANK YOU.

I WANT PEOPLE WHO WANT TO SPEND THEIR DAYS WITH MY TEAM, MY COMPANIES AND ME. PEOPLE WHO ARE JUST AS PASSIONATE AND CAFFEINATED AS I AM. PEOPLE WHO ARE WILLING TO GO TO THE MOUNTAIN FOR ME. FIGHT THE GOOD FIGHT.

WE HAVE TO BE OKAY WITH RELEASING THEM FOR OTHER OPPORTUNITIES.

Sometimes it's a blessing. Maybe you loved the person but not their behaviors. Maybe they were holding you back with their lack of commitment, drive or focus.

Sometimes you have to be the one to let people go, to release them when the time is clear.

People fire themselves. When they don't do the work, have the wrong behaviors or attitudes, are negative, slow, and don't drink the Kool-Aid for your mission, your company, your culture.

Release them for other opportunities.

Recently, a teammate I truly admire gave his notice. I was beyond surprised. He told me he felt that his leader didn't appreciate him, he felt like he had zero chance to grow or the possibility for more pay. He was wrong. We had all those things for him.

We just forgot to tell him. We also forgot to ask him what he needed or wanted in order to be his best with us.

We will do better next time. Self-evaluate your role in the hiring, the training, the communication, the lack of connection to your mission, your leadership.

When I see people leave for the wrong reasons, it reminds me of a card I keep on my desk at home: **Happiness is wanting what you have.**

When your people do leave, do me a favor: Wish them well and mean it.

You never know when you will see them again. I have had some of the best people leave for one reason or another and come back.

BE CURIOUS.
KEEP LEARNING.
TAKE ACTION.
FAIL OR SUCCEED.
MEASURE,
ADJUST.
REPEAT.

—TAI LOPEZ

LET'S GO

TAKE ACTION TO BE BETTER.

YOU GO FIRST.

1.

REALIZE: PEOPLE QUIT.

2.

LOVINGLY RELEASE THE ONES
THAT AREN'T MEANT FOR YOU.

3.

ALLOW PEOPLE TO COME BACK.

CHAPTER 9

COME IN, HOUSTON

Communication—the human connection—is the key to personal and career success.

—Paul J. Meyer

Recently, my son was being recruited by several Division I college hockey coaches. I loved watching the communication between my son and all of the different coaches.

I learned so much and confirmed what I had imagined to be true:

COMMUNICATION = CONNECTION

ATTENTION = QUALITY

The coach who communicated the most WON. He was the coach who sent the most texts, called the most, came to see him play the most, showed a genuine interest in him. He was the coach who successfully recruited my son to play hockey for him.

Another coach barely touched base with my son, never texted or called, never attended a game in person, relying only on tapes. That coach lost.

PEOPLE WANT TO HAVE A CONNECTION WITH THEIR LEADERS. THEY WANT TO KNOW THEIR LEADERS CARE, THAT THEY ARE INVESTED, THAT THEY ARE ALL IN.

Holding regular one on ones with my team is a must. These are followed up with 15-minute quarterly reviews with each team member. We review our growth plan, their goals and vision for the next quarter.

A SAMPLE 15-MINUTE QUARTERLY CHECK-IN SHEET CAN BE FOUND AT
DOWNLOADS.YOUGOFIRST.COM

If you go with the 15-minute quarterly check-in, your one-year reviews are actually effective and help to keep you and your team connected. We need to talk more often, tweak, adjust, give love, give thanks and make sure we are on the same page, all heading in the same direction.

GET UP OUT OF YOUR CHAIR AND WALK AROUND. CHECK ON THE VIBE OF YOUR TEAM. SAY HELLO OR GOOD MORNING. GET CRAZY! HUG SOMEONE, HIGH FIVE THEM, CHECK IN, ASK QUESTIONS, SAY THANK YOU.

PEOPLE WANT TO BE AFFIRMED.

I was asked to speak to a local varsity high school football team here in the valley last year. The team was getting ready to compete in the semifinals for the state tournament. This team had never beaten the team it was set to play in the semifinals, and the opponent they would most likely face IF they won the semis would be the team they lost to earlier in the year.

I was asked to inspire them to win a state championship.

The first thing I did was study their game films. I watched several of their games and also the game films from the other team. I was looking for connection between the coaches and their players. I was watching how the coaches held themselves, what the culture was like, the feeling on the field. Then I came up with the three things this team was going to need if they were going to win it all.

/. The first thing I noticed was that the players and coaches only high fived, hugged, or showed any passion *after* they scored. There were no atta boys or words of encouragement if something went wrong. The sidelines and the field were quiet.

2. The second thing I noticed was that based on their past losses to both teams, our team had no **belief** they could actually win.

3. The third thing was the need for physical **grind**—the team that works the hardest would prevail.

I spent 30 minutes with them. The entire time, a favorite song—"Pure Grind"— blared in the background. I just looped it over and over again. I asked them several questions and had them chant/yell the answers to me:

DID YOU WORK HARD TO GET HERE? *THEY SHOUTED:* **YES!**

WILL YOU WIN A STATE CHAMPIONSHIP? *THEY SHOUTED:* **YES!**

DO YOU BELIEVE IN YOUR TEAM? *THEY SHOUTED:* **YES!**

Then we talked about the importance of touches during a game. I needed the players and coaches to high five, inspire, motivate, push when they screwed up or when things weren't going their way. I wanted them to add a whole new dimension to their game.

They needed to believe. I told them if they kept asking themselves the questions above and answering with a resounding YES and supported each other on the field on game day, they would win.

I then shared with them my song at the end of our time together. And my thoughts on talent and hard work.

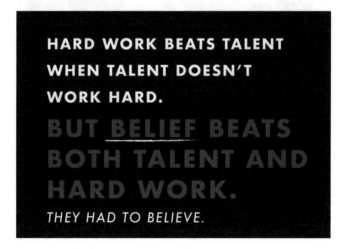

HARD WORK BEATS TALENT WHEN TALENT DOESN'T WORK HARD.

BUT BELIEF BEATS BOTH TALENT AND HARD WORK.

THEY HAD TO BELIEVE.

They all worked hard, they all had talent. They just needed to throw a little belief into the mix. And that started with the coaches.

Spoiler alert.

They won both games. They became the state champions.

They had a connection. They believed in their team and their coaches, and they all shared a common goal.

YES!

STATE CHAMPS!

Do you know how your team is feeling?

Do they believe?

Are they excited?

Or are they burned out?

Do they think you are doing a good job?

What do they think you could do better?

HERE ARE THREE QUESTIONS YOU NEED TO ASK YOUR TEAM ON A REGULAR BASIS:

1. What are they feeling?

2. What are they thinking?

3. What do they need to be successful?

Chris Guillebeau, the author of *The Art of Nonconformity*, said there is a simple thing you can do to improve any relationship—to become a better leader, friend, partner or spouse. He writes:

"Figure out what they want to do, to become,

or achieve and then help them do it. Don't

do it for them—it's their dream, after all—but

show interest and offer tangible support.

How can you do that today? How can you make a connection? Figure it out and see what happens to your relationship.

Now, let's talk about you as a leader. How do you watch your game films? What's it like to be coached by you?

I am a huge fan of author Gary Vaynerchuk. I have read his books and follow him on Twitter. He is not for the weak of heart. He recently commented on the urgency for self-awareness as you lead your team. He taught me that success requires a combination of things, including self-awareness, hustle and understanding the difference between **"the clouds and the dirt."**

THE CLOUDS ARE THE PIE IN THE SKY. THEY ARE ALL THE THINGS YOU DREAM OF. WHAT YOU HOPE FOR, WHAT YOU WANT BUT DON'T QUITE HAVE.

THE DIRT IS THE HARD WORK, THE GRIT, THE DOING, THE WORKING LATE, THE GOING IN EARLY TO MAKE YOUR DREAMS COME TRUE.

In order to succeed, Vaynerchuk contends, you need to create an environment where those around you can tell you like it is—what you are good at and what you are not so good at.

I sat down with one of the leaders on my team and I asked him to give me an honest assessment of my leadership skills and what he thought I could improve on. I knew he would be honest with me. He trusted me. He trusted that I wouldn't hold his comments against him, and that I would use his words to improve. He told me that he loves my positivity, my drive, my belief in him and my team. He then took a deep breath and said he wished I would slow down sometimes. It is so clear to you where we are going, BUT it is not clear to us. We would like more information on what's out in front, on what we see. He said he doesn't always agree with or understand the choices I make.

MAN, this was good for me. A reminder to slow down, share my vision, better explain the process, the next steps and where we are going. You want your employees to feel safe doing this—or it will never happen. This means sometimes hearing things that you disagree with or even upset you. **Your job is to listen to the feedback and thank them for bringing it to you.**

Once you have listened to the feedback, it's time to start focusing your energy on the things that you are good at and delegating the things that you're not so good at.

EXERCISE:

SIT DOWN WITH 5 OF YOUR EMPLOYEES AND ASK THEM TO GIVE YOU AN HONEST ASSESSMENT OF YOUR LEADERSHIP AND ABILITY. ASK THEM WHERE YOU ARE STRONG AND WHERE YOU ARE WEAK. THEN, AFTER LISTENING TO THEIR FEEDBACK, TELL THEM WHAT YOU INTEND TO DO ABOUT IT

(FOCUSING MORE TIME ON YOUR STRENGTHS, DELEGATING YOUR WEAKNESSES).

I LOVE MEETING WITH MY TEAMS. I WANT TO HEAR FROM THEM. WHAT'S WORKING, WHAT'S NOT, WHO'S WORKING, WHO'S NOT.

For your next meeting with your team, I want you to do a meeting/communication audit. Have someone who does not need to be in the meeting join your meeting. Their job is to keep track of who's sharing, who's talking and who's not. It can be done by drawing a picture of the table and the chair configuration of the meeting, putting each person's name at their respective chairs. Every time someone talks a line is drawn from the speaker to the middle of the table or to the person their comments were directed to.

At the end you should have lines going from each person to the middle, to the leader and to other teammates. **The point is you want discussion, collaboration.** If the line is only from the leader to the team, you are not collaborating and sharing with your team. You are a dictator.

COMMUNICATION **EQUALS** CONNECTION.

GET THEM TALKING AND SHARING.

REMIND THEM THAT THEY ARE NEEDED.

John Maxwell keeps 10 blank note cards at his desk every Monday morning and by the end of the week, he will have sent them to 10 people, noting the things they are good at, how they are succeeding. Try it. Thank your team, your clients, your vendors, your family, the people who help you. If you want higher-quality relationships, a higher level of connection, then **you go first.**

Reach out and communicate.

Your team is waiting.

LET'S GO

TAKE ACTION TO BE BETTER.

YOU GO FIRST.

1.

AUDIT YOUR CURRENT LEVEL OF
COMMUNICATION WITH YOUR
TEAM. HOW OFTEN DO YOU
MEET? TALK? SEE EACH OTHER?

2.

ASK YOUR TEAM MEMBERS WHAT
THEY ARE FEELING, WHAT THEY
ARE THINKING, WHAT THEY
NEED TO BE SUCCESSFUL.

3.

DO THE SELF-AWARENESS EXERCISE
BY GARY VAYNERCHUK.

CHAPTER 10

YOUR JOB IS TO MAKE THINGS BETTER

You must realize that leaders lead from the front. Your job is to make things better. Recently I attended Darren Hardy's High Performance Forum, where, for two-and-a-half days, 75 business leaders and owners from around the globe learned the five things a leader must do every day:

1. **Set the pace.**
2. **Clear obstacles.**
3. **Get needed resources.**
4. **Grow the team/company faster.**
5. **Be out front.**

THE CLIFFNOTES VERSION:

MAKE THINGS BETTER.

Side note, I almost didn't attend the High Performance Forum. I was busy and felt like I should put it off or not attend at all. Darren Hardy opened the class by saying, "Thank you for attending, please turn off your cell phones and be all-in for the next two days. And if you can't be away from your team or company for two days then you must be a shitty leader." That was like a punch in the nose. He was right; I needed to be there to be better for my team and myself.

A LEADER MUST EAT CHANGE FOR BREAKFAST.

Expect it. Anticipate it. Go around it, under it, above it. When someone tells me they don't like change, it's a major red flag to me. How can they lead a team, a company or themselves if they want everything to stay the same?

You are either moving forward or backward. There is no in between.

LEADERS FIGHT FOR BETTER.

FIGHT FOR CHANGE BECAUSE YOUR TEAM KNOWS THAT CHANGE = PROGRESS.

Kat Cole, the Group President of Focus Brands (think Cinnabon), shared her hotshot rule concept at Leadercast last year in Atlanta. The hotshot rule is an exercise that Cole does every quarter. She thinks like a new, young, aggressive hotshot. If she was a hotshot in her position at Focus Brands, what are the three things they would do? WOW. Mind blown. She realizes that if we do the same things day in and day out we get complacent. We drink our own Kool-Aid and forget to look outside ourselves to audit our attitude, actions and progress.

TRY IT. IF A NEW PERSON TOOK OVER YOUR POSITION, WHAT THREE THINGS WOULD THEY DO DIFFERENTLY? BETTER?

1.

2.

3.

One of my favorite movies of all time is *The Martian* with Matt Damon. There were 13 life lessons in the movie that clearly demonstrated his leadership skills.

1. You must believe in yourself and then you must NEVER stop believing.

2. Have a Plan B, Plan C, Plan D and so on.

3. Be really smart.

4. When you give a time frame to complete a job...you can do better. Give more effort.

5. Ship it, even if it's not perfect.

6. Look at the horizon every day. Be thankful you're alive.

7. Have no regrets.

8. Fight to live.

9. Use all the brainpower surrounding you. It's gonna take the whole damn team.

10. Leave no man behind.

11. It takes a lot of WORK to have success.

12. Become a teacher, share your knowledge and all you have learned.

13. Life comes down to the ability to keep solving problems.

Number 13 is pure leadership magic. It should read: **Leadership comes down to the ability to keep solving problems.** When you solve problems you make your team, your company, your life BETTER.

How do I deal with problems? I devour them. I love problems. I do. It means that I'm leading, pushing, solving and making us BETTER. TALK DIRTY.

STRATEGY NO. 1:

IS THAT ALL YOU GOT?

You need to expect problems and eat them for breakfast. As they are flying toward you, your email, your phone, a text, a person at your office door. Man up, listen, think, solve and move on to the next problem.

Next time someone throws you a curveball, a real humdinger of a problem, add some swagger to your walk and then say to them, **"Is that all you got?" Then wink.**

STRATEGY NO. 2:

WOULD IT HELP?

The most important question you must ask yourself in the middle of a crisis, in the middle of problems, when you are staring at the person bringing you the problem is

"WILL MY REACTION HELP OR HINDER MY ABILITY OR MY TEAM'S ABILITY TO SOLVE THIS PROBLEM?"

Am I making things BETTER or worse with my attitude? Myers Barnes, a good friend of mine, says it best: "The problem isn't the problem. It's your attitude toward the problem." Let other people throw fits, yell, scream, shout, etc. Not you.

YOU'RE A LEADER. YOU ARE HERE TO MAKE THINGS BETTER.

STRATEGY NO. 3:

THINK YES!

Be clear. This is my favorite word in the English dictionary. Think about it. In every movie when things go wrong, the first word you hear out of the actor's mouth is:

NOOOOOOOOOOOOOOOOOOOOOOOO

OOOOOOOOOOOOOOOOOOOOOOO!!!!

Not us, not anymore.

From now on you are going to focus on **YES!** This one word catches people totally off guard. Instead of losing it, you rise to the occasion and offer a positive spin:

YES, I love
this problem.

YES, I can hardly
wait to dive in.

YES, I love challenges.

YES, this is awesome.

YES, of course.

Pick your favorite strategy and get to it. Your
team needs you to show the way. They want to
be better.

YOUR JOB IS PROGRESSION NOT PERFECTION.

MAKE PROGRESS.
KEEP MOVING
FORWARD.

Let's flip the coin and talk about what needs to be done once you have solved all the problems and issues flying your way. You get to dive into coming up with new ideas and strategies that move your team forward. I firmly believe that I read way too many Curious George books as a child. I have a million questions, I want to know why, who, what, when, why did you do it that way, why not this way, how come and so many more.

BE CURIOUS ALWAYS. FOR KNOWLEDGE WILL NOT ACQUIRE YOU—YOU MUST ACQUIRE IT. —SUDIE BACK

Each quarter I reach out to the members of my company and ask them to share ideas with me that would make us better. We get hundreds of submissions. Not only is this amazing, but it shows that you are not meant to do this alone. Reach out to your team. Listen and implement.

GO TO CONFERENCES, WATCH WEBINARS, LISTEN TO PODCASTS, READ, READ AND READ SOME MORE. THERE IS INSPIRATION ALL AROUND YOU. BRAINSTORM WITH OTHER LEADERS IN OTHER PROFESSIONS. ATTEND CONFERENCES OUT OF YOUR INDUSTRY. HEAR FRESH PERSPECTIVES. ALL THESE HELP YOU LEAN TOWARD WINNING.

Know what else will help you win? Scoreboards, dashboards, numbers and that leadership word we all dream of: accountability. Are you watching the numbers? Do you have a system in place that shows you quickly and easily if you and your team are winning or losing? There should be no mystery nor should you be clueless about what areas need improvement.

Be fanatic about the scoreboard. Watch what's important and then constantly tweak to make things better. Are you watching the right things? Every Monday morning I get a down-dirty dashboard of numbers for the week prior. They cover every area of the company. Then, throughout the month, I look at the score of each department. At the end of the month I look at the scoreboard as a whole. Then, each quarter, our company comes together to review the scoreboard.

Your team needs to know if they are winning or losing. They need to know what they are doing is working, or if they are losing they need to be told by YOU what needs to be done to make things better.

Be on the hunt for better because I can promise you it won't come looking for you. Leaders go get it. Are you out in front or in the trenches?

You must get out in front. Your team needs you. They don't need perfection. That is a pipe dream. They just need progress. They need better. I am so passionate about better that I wrote a book about it, called *Better Human: It's a Full-Time Job.*

Your team should fully understand that you want them to be better. When you hire them be sure they are coachable, growth orientated and understand the need to be better. You want people around you who have this hunger for more, for better.

A LEADER'S NO. 1 JOB IS TO MAKE THINGS BETTER. IT'S A FULL-TIME JOB.

LET'S GO

TAKE ACTION TO BE BETTER.

YOU GO FIRST.

1.

TRY OUT KAT COLE'S
HOTSHOT RULE EXERCISE.

2.

EMBRACE ONE OF MY STRATEGIES
THE NEXT TIME A PROBLEM COMES
YOUR WAY, ASKING YOURSELF:
IS THAT ALL I'VE GOT?

3.

ASK YOUR TEAM FOR IDEAS ON
HOW TO MAKE YOUR COMPANY
OR PRODUCT BETTER.

CHAPTER 11

LOVE WINS

A couple of years ago I sent out my annual company survey to my team of over 100 employees and I asked them to offer some feedback on the past year. I wanted their opinion about what worked, what didn't and what we could be doing better. An obvious theme emerged from their answers: **LOVE. Yes, love.**

They loved our success, our events, our processes and our homes. They loved their job, their family and their team. There was so much love, in fact, we decided that "love wins" would be our company theme that year. When you love who you are, what you do, your clients, your vendors, your team and your company, you win, too.

EVERY
TIME.

IT BEATS FEAR, ANGER, DOUBT,
LAZY, SLOW AND MEAN.

It's that simple. If you hate your job, your company, your team, yourself—you're done for. You know the feeling: You are at a restaurant or a store and the employee looks like they are being tortured, so of course, they take it out on you.

That's not winning. That's not love. In fact, I have a secret for you:

THE MORE YOU LOVE, THE HARDER YOU WORK.

One of my favorite moments in leadership, love and winning was at the end of the 2016 National College Football Championship between the Alabama Crimson Tide and the Clemson Tigers. Clemson won the game, which was a HUGE victory—the game ended, the crowd went wild, thousands of people rushed the field, confetti flew. A reporter stuck a microphone in the face of Coach Dabo Swinney of the Clemson Tigers and asked this:

How did they do it?

How did you beat the best team in the country?

He said, **"The difference in the game tonight is...love. My word all year for my guys has been love. Because we love each other we will win this game."**

TO VIEW THIS VIDEO, CHECK OUT
DOWNLOADS.YOUGOFIRST.COM

He was right.

I was watching the game with my family when this interview came on and, needless to say, I went nuts. I was jumping up and down and fist pumping. He gets it. Dabo Swinney gets it.

STILL NOT WITH ME ON THIS WHOLE LOVE THING?

Let's head on over to the sounds of the NFL and look up the 2017 Super Bowl game with the Patriots, Tom Brady and the Atlanta Falcons. They were losing—losing badly. But if you watch the clips, you can overhear Tom Brady telling his guys he loves them. No matter what happens he loves them. They pulled out that win against some serious odds.

WHEN YOU'RE LOVED, WHEN SOMEONE BELIEVES IN YOU, IT'S A GAME CHANGER.

I LOVE WHAT I DO, I LOVE MY TEAM, I LOVE MY COMPANY, I LOVE ME. GAME CHANGERS, ALL OF THEM.

HOW ABOUT YOU?

As a leader, you go first. Show your team how much you love them, how much you love what you do, how much you love your company. It's important.

It's easy to focus on the negative, it's easy to criticize, and it's easy to be selfish. Don't fall into that style of leadership. Each person you come in contact with has a sign hanging around their neck that says

"I need love."

Isn't that what you want? Love is the secret you've all been waiting for. Your leadership style, your team and your performance will never be the same if you focus on love.

But don't take my word for it. Let's talk about wildly successful companies that focus on the good. Companies that love what they do and who they serve. They are called the Firms of Endearment. These companies are fueled by passion and purpose...**by love.**

Amazon

CarMax

Chipotle

Costco

FedEx

Google

Harley-Davidson

Marriott International

New Balance

Nordstrom

Panera

Patagonia

Southwest Airlines

Starbucks

TOMS

Trader Joe's

Walt Disney

Whole Foods Market

SUCCESS LEAVES TRACKS.

Need I say more? This list is made up of well respected, wildly popular, deeply loved brands.

If you want to learn more about Firms of Endearment, read *Firms of Endearment: How World-Class Companies Profit from Passion and Purpose* by Rajendra S. Sisodia, Jagdish N. Sheth and David B. Wolfe.

In the movie *Jerry McGuire*, Cuba Gooding Jr.'s character tells Tom Cruise's character to yell

SHOW ME THE MONEY!

Do you realize that when employees were asked what the five most important things were, **money was ranked fifth?!**

He should have yelled:

SHOW ME THE LOVE!

MEET WITH YOUR TEAM, HAVE REGULAR ONE ON ONES, FIND OUT ABOUT THEIR LIFE. WHAT ARE THEY FOCUSED ON? WHAT CAN YOU HELP WITH? *CARE, LISTEN, LOVE THEM AND THEY WILL DO THE SAME FOR YOU, FOR YOUR TEAM AND YOUR COMPANY.*

THESE ARE THE MOST IMPORTANT MEETINGS I HAVE. THEY GIVE ME *(AND YOU!)* A CHANCE TO BUILD RELATIONSHIPS, TO LEARN ABOUT WHAT'S GOING ON IN THEIR LIFE AT WORK AND AT HOME, TO DISCUSS ISSUES, TO HELP SOLVE PROBLEMS, TO HEAR NEW IDEAS AND TO TALK ABOUT THEIR GOALS.

THIS MEETING HELPS DETERMINE, ON A SCALE OF 1 TO 10, HOW HAPPY THEY ARE.

ARE THEY LOVING WHAT THEY ARE DOING?

Channel Curious George and ask some questions (and, of course, listen more than talk):

1. If you had one suggestion for us to improve, what would it be?

2. What's the number one problem with our company?

3. What do you like the least about working here?

4. If you were me, what changes would you make?

5. What do you think is the least useful feature in our product?

6. What's the biggest marketing opportunity that we should be doing?

7. Are you happy working here?

8. What do you think are your three biggest strengths?

TAKE NOTES AND THEN TAKE ACTION.

Your team gives you 40 to 60 hours of hard work each week. How about you giving them an hour?

If you were to visit me at my office and spend the day with us, you could expect:

To hear the words...**I love you.**

To witness people hugging.

To come across a one-on-one meeting. They happen often and at every level.

To read our motto **"Love"** written on our walls.

To see pictures of our team together, happy, full of **love.**

To read testimonials from our buyers sharing the **love.**

We have been voted one of the best places to work in Idaho the last five years. Our team voted anonymously and with a third party. My heart swells. This year at our company kick-off, we gave all the gentlemen on the team a Love Wins tee and the ladies received Love Wins necklaces. WE BELIEVE IN LOVE. WE ARE ALL IN.

MY NEXT GOAL? GET ON THE FIRMS OF ENDEARMENT LIST.

LOVE
WINS

EVERY
TIME

LET'S GO

TAKE ACTION TO BE BETTER.

YOU GO FIRST.

1.

WATCH THE DABO SWINNEY
VIDEO ON LOVE.

2.

RESEARCH THE COMPANIES THAT
MADE THE FIRMS OF ENDEARMENT
LIST AND WHAT MAKES THEM
GREAT. THEN GO DO THAT.

3.

SCHEDULE ONE-ON-ONE
MEETINGS WITH YOUR TEAM.

CHAPTER 12

FILL YOUR TANK

Education is the mother

of leadership.

–Wendell Willkie

I am often asked about my life, and how I get things done. People ask:

What's your morning ritual?
How do you keep your drive and energy?
Do you ever get burned out?
How do you balance it all?
How do you motivate others?
What are your favorite books?
How do you remain positive
in a negative situation?
Why are you so passionate?
How do you inspire others?
What is your best attribute as a leader?

The answer to all of these is easy:
I fill my tank. Daily.

As a leader, you spend your days emptying your
tank. You are busy solving problems, helping
others to greatness, thinking, planning, working
hard. To do this takes work. You have to keep
adding new knowledge, new fuel and new ideas.
How? One way is to read.

I am a ferocious reader. Definition of ferocious:
intense, strong, powerful, fierce, severe, extreme,
acute, unbearable, raging; hellish. Pretty much

sums up how I feel about reading. On average the top leaders of the world read five books a week. No, that wasn't a typo. Five books. Each week. It's how you fill your tank.

Are you cringing because you don't have time to read, or really just don't enjoy it? Sign up for Audible.com and listen instead. While you drive. While you eat. Make the time. We need you to be better.

You HAVE TO GO FIRST.

Your team, your company can only go as far as your leadership and your current knowledge. You need to be in front of all of them. You matter the most. Why? You can't help people with their greatest potential until you're in the process of reaching your own. The number one constraint to the growth of any organization is the leader.

Are you holding everyone back or inspiring your team to be better?

If you knew better, you'd do better. In order for any of us to hit our goals and become the person we dream about, we need to educate ourselves.

RING THE BELL.

SCHOOL'S IN.

There are a few things I read/watch every morning in order to start my day and to make sure I am moving forward:

1. **Dd.darrenhardy.com:** Darren Daily. A quick video for achievers by Darren Hardy.

2. **Jongordon.com:** Developing positive people, leaders, organizations and teams.

3. **Startwithwhy.com:** Simon Sinek's simple but powerful model for inspirational leadership.

4. **Medium.com:** I follow authors who write about leadership. My favorite author is Benjamin Hardy.

5. I send out my **Better Thinking** quote each morning. I do it for me, but would love for you to join me. **Go to www.betterhuman.today** and sign up. Two years ago I decided to pick my top 50 quotes and inspirations and bring them to life with artwork to publish my second book, *Better Thinking: Think Better, Be Better.*

My intent was to fill my tank so that I could fill the tanks of those around me.

I also make sure to attend leadership conferences and listen to speakers every chance I get.

FILL YOUR TANK WITH BOOKS, PODCASTS, BLOGS, DAILY QUOTES, CONFERENCES—THEN PAY IT FORWARD BY SHARING YOUR NEWLY ACQUIRED KNOWLEDGE WITH YOUR TEAM.

BREAK UP WITH FACEBOOK, SNAPCHAT, TWITTER AND INSTAGRAM. **YOU NEED TO FOCUS ON GROWTH, LEADERSHIP, POSITIVE ENERGY, THINGS THAT PUSH YOU TO BE BETTER, NOT THINGS THAT HAVE THE POTENTIAL TO BRING YOU DOWN.**

PLAN YOUR DAYS. PLAN YOUR LIFE.

IN ORDER TO HAVE THE BALANCE WE ALL CRAVE, YOU HAVE TO DECIDE WHAT'S IMPORTANT AND WHAT YOU NEED TO BE AN EFFECTIVE LEADER.

You don't have a time management problem; you have a **self-management** problem.

—*Darren Hardy*

You have time to read, to watch a video, to attend a leadership conference and still enjoy your life. It's a simple matter of making the decision and putting it on your calendar.

A good friend of mine once said to me, "Ronda, you are the most important meeting you have each day."

Want to fill your family time tank? **Schedule it.**

Want to get healthy? **Schedule it.**

Want to meditate? **Schedule it.**

Want to go on vacation? **Schedule it.**

Want to read every morning? **Schedule it.**

My entire life is on my calendar. If it's important to me, to my success, to my sanity, it's on my calendar. We all have the same amount of time. Fill your days with things that fill your tank.

I know you know all of this. I just want to know if you're doing any of it?

When you love what you do, your team and your career, your tank is filled by your team's successes and by the love you feel each day by being a part of such an amazing company. I want this for you.

The most powerful thing is that you are a leader. You can have all of this. Get out there.

FILL YOUR TANK

THE WORLD NEEDS MORE OF YOU IN IT.

LET'S GO

TAKE ACTION TO BE BETTER.

YOU GO FIRST.

1.

SIGN UP FOR A DAILY QUOTE,
BLOG, VIDEO, ETC. *SEE MY LIST*.

2.

FIND AT LEAST ONE LEADERSHIP
CONFERENCE TO ATTEND THIS YEAR.

3.

REVIEW YOUR SCHEDULE EVERY DAY.
PLAN YOUR DAYS. PLAN YOUR LIFE.

CHAPTER 13

THANK YOU AND PLEASE COME BACK TOMORROW

My crew works hard. They do. At times I can be demanding, relentless, overwhelming and push just a little too hard. It's in my nature. I want people around me who get it. Who want to be better.

I remember one evening around 7:30 p.m.: My personal cheerleader was leaving the office after several long days and as she said goodnight, I said, "THANK YOU AND PLEASE COME BACK TOMORROW." I couldn't imagine my life if she didn't come back. If she left because she didn't realize how important she is to me—how much I need her smarts, her work ethic, her drive and her attitude. She is a HUGE part of my success.

I say that to everyone in my life. Not just my office crew. I say it to my husband and my kids. I want them to come back tomorrow. I want them to know how grateful I am for them in my life.

HOW OFTEN DO YOU OFFER YOUR THANKS TO YOUR TEAM?

DO YOU ASK THEM TO COME BACK TOMORROW? *AND THE NEXT DAY? AND THE NEXT?*

HAVE YOU TOLD THEM HOW **GLAD YOU ARE THAT THEY ARE HERE?**

I will add one more Rondaism to this mix. On birthdays I try to make a point to reach out and tell the people in my life that I am so glad they were born. I AM. I am blessed they are in my life, a part of my journey, helping me on my way to world domination.

Be thankful they are pouring their hearts and minds out each day. People need to understand how important they are. I love the African proverb that says, **"If you want to go fast, go alone. If you want to go far, go together."** If you want to have and do more, you need AMAZING people with you, working hard, every day. They need to feel like their work matters. That they are important to you, the mission, the team and the company. You couldn't do it without them. People love to feel needed. And they need a purpose—a why to keep coming back.

We take it for granted that people on our team will come back every day. That is, until they don't. Four simple words at the end of your day are all you need: PLEASE COME BACK TOMORROW.

MAGIC, I TELL YOU. MAGIC.

We work this magic throughout the year and in dozens of ways. A couple times a year, for example, we set up a gratitude jar in our kitchen at the office. We put little white pieces of paper and pens next to it, and for two weeks we ask the team to fill out all the things we are grateful for. **A jar full of blessings. A jar full of love.** And then we share all the things we are grateful for at our quarterly company meetings. It helps keep us focused on the right things. If you are the leader of a big organization, you can ask for emails noting those things your team is thankful for. Then choose a few to be read in company meetings or events.

ONLY THINGS MORE POWERFUL THAN <u>SEX</u> AND <u>MONEY</u> ARE PRAISE AND RECOGNITION.

—MARY KAY ASH

PRAISE AND RECOGNITION.

WE ALL WANT THEM. WE ALL NEED THEM. WE NEED TO BE AFFIRMED WE ARE ON THE RIGHT PATH, DOING THE RIGHT THINGS.

DON'T BE SHY WITH THE PRAISE.

Break out the megahorn and tell the world. Simply put, we praise and recognize the people and companies we do business with. Start with your team. Give them the praise and recognition they need to fill their tanks. Encourage other departments, other teams to give **love and recognition** to other teams.

One of my favorite team exercises is to tape a white piece of paper on each person's back and then have everyone go around and write what they love about each person on the paper. Give everyone about 15 minutes. The room gets loud, people are sharing, laughing and pouring love into those sheets. When you're done, the teammate gets to keep their paper to remind them why everyone thinks they are so delicious and loved.

Do you share your reviews? Do you share positive feedback? Please do. It's important. It's part of the why that fuels us all to come back.

Leaders grow. They are not made.
—Peter Drucker

We need people to come back tomorrow so we can continue to help them grow into leaders. This is the final truth of what it means to be a leader. You have an obligation to raise up those in your care. Bring your team with you on this journey. I share every book, conference, blog and podcast with my team and my family. I want them all to come with me. I want them all to be leaders.

THANK YOU FOR INVESTING IN YOURSELF AND FOR GOING FIRST, FOR SHOWING THE WAY WITH YOUR ATTITUDE, ACTIONS AND RESULTS...AND FOR DOING IT EVERY DAY. YOU INSPIRE ME.

BRING ALL THE PASSION YOU CAN MUSTER UP, EMPTY THE TANK AND, FOR THE LOVE OF PETE, HAVE SOME FUN. THIS HAPPENS WHEN YOU LOVE WHAT YOU DO, WHO YOU ARE, YOUR TEAM, YOUR COMPANY, YOUR FAMILY, YOUR FRIENDS. LOVE WINS. EVERY TIME.

BE A LEADER OF LEADERS.

YOU GO FIRST.

LET'S GO

TAKE ACTION TO BE BETTER.

YOU GO FIRST.

1.

TELL YOUR TEAM THANK YOU AND
PLEASE COME BACK TOMORROW.

2.

SET UP A GRATITUDE JAR
FOR YOUR TEAM.

3.

DO THE WHITE PAPER ACTIVITY.

Now What?

One of my favorite things to do after I read a book or attend a conference is to put all the ideas and actions I loved on sticky notes. Then I post them on my wall. As I complete each item I take it down. It helps me stay focused on making things happen, on implementing what I learned.

The "Let's Go" list at the end of each chapter is to inspire you. To push you to think differently.

Share this with your team. Grow together.

Visit my site **www.yougofirst.com.** I want to help you on your leadership journey. Sign up for monthly videos, my leadership monthly subscription box and more. You are on your way to becoming the leader you wish you had. It's a full-time job, but one you can handle.

If you want to know how this whole journey started for me, read my two other books: *Better Human* and *Better Thinking*.

Drop me a line at: ronda@betterhuman.today and tell me your favorite leadership story.

Just like you, I am far from done.

LET'S

Acknowledgments

THANKS TO JIM CONGER, my rock, my husband. His love, support and unwavering belief in me has been the inspiration I needed to write this book. My love for him is in overwhelming proportions. MY SONS inspire me to be better every day. They are destined for greatness and I hope that I make them proud. BABS, my stepmother, was sent to me from the heavens and for that I will be forever grateful. She has taught me how to prevail no matter the circumstances. Thanks to my AUNT BETTY AND UNCLE JOE for showing me how to be a leader when it comes to family. They have led the way with their love, their ability to always give, and with their love for each other. Thank you for showing me the way.

TARA AND HOLLY have been by my side for the last 18 years. They've been with me every step of the way. They are my wingmen, yes-men, partners in crime and dear friends. Once again, they jumped on board to help me write this book. They edit, add, cheer me on and push me to be better. Most of all, I am thankful for their unconditional love.

To CECE CHENEY, my word magician, one of my favorite yes-girls, and personal deejay. You're so much fun and I love you.

To COREY BARTON, thank you for being a fearless leader. Thank you for sharing your company with me. I will be forever grateful for spending my days at CBH Homes with such an amazing team. You mean the world to me and I can't wait for what the future holds for CBH.

To THE ALOHA CREW, thank you for making this book possible. So glad you are here. You are all delicious and I love you. MARYANNA, I love everything your company stands for. More importantly, I love your energy, spirit and belief in me. ANNA, I completely understand it's been a full-time job being my editor. You make me better. I love you madly and thank you for being so damn talented.

To my magical designer of all things beautiful, ARIELLE HEINONEN. Once again, you have brought my book and my vision to life. I will be forever grateful.

To my readers: I love you.
I love hearing your stories, your cards, your emails, your messages. I read every one. Thanks for filling my tank.

About the Author

Some say she was raised by wolves, others claim truckers. No matter what her upbringing, this super woman has flourished in a male dominated industry for 24 years. Beginning in the wild, wild West of Las Vegas in 1993 with KB Homes, a top five national homebuilder, Ronda Conger has staked her claim as the Vice President of Idaho's largest homebuilder, CBH Homes, where she leads the CBH troops daily, overseeing all areas of the company for the past 14 years.

Her resume doesn't stop there. Recently, Ronda was named a 2017 Constructech Women in Construction award recipient, comprised of some of the most successful women working within construction in the nation. Ronda currently serves as a board member of the St. Luke's Children's Hospital, board of directors member for the Treasure Valley YMCA, Library Leader for the Boise Public Library, and is a Together Treasure Valley partner. She happily gives back as an active member of the Treasure Valley business community.

As a business woman, professional speaker and author, Ronda is on a mission to spread a movement with her award-winning books: *Better Human: It's a Full-Time Job* and *Better Thinking: Think Better. Be Better*, and now: *You Go First: Become the Leader Your Team Needs*.

It's been rumored her high energy and passion come from shotgunning Red Bulls daily, but she'll tell you it comes from her incredibly hot husband, Jim Conger (just ask her), and her two sons.

She thanks the heavens each day for this incredible journey and is so very grateful for the opportunity to serve and love all those that she comes in contact with.